Poetry Pond

Also by Jennifer Chrystie and published by Ginninderra Press
Polishing the Silver
The Weight of Snow

Jennifer Chrystie
Poetry Pond

Acknowledgements

Some of these poems were first published in
Poems 2013, volume 2 of the Australian Poetry Ltd Members' Anthology
Shot Glass Journal (USA), issues 8, 9, 13, 16, 22, 25 and 30
Poam issue 364, Melbourne Poets Union
Cancer Council arts catalogue, 2013
Lightness of Being, Poetica Christi anthology, 2014
Imagine, Poetica Christi anthology, 2015
Love's Footprint, Poetica Christi anthology, 2019
First Refuge, Ginninderra Press edited by Anne Nadge, 2016
Poetry Monash 90, Winter 2015
Studio, number 132, 2014

Many thanks to the Nandina poets and to my publisher,
Stephen Matthews

Poetry Pond
ISBN 978 1 76109 070 7
Copyright © Jennifer Chrystie 2021

First published 2021 by
GINNINDERRA PRESS
PO Box 3461 Port Adelaide 5015 Australia
www.ginninderrapress.com.au

Contents

On the Brink	9
Creation	10
Waiting for the Muse	11
Poetry Pond	12
Blown Away	13
Memory Quilt	14
The Family Tree	15
Seven Mothers	16
The Iceman	18
The Lady and the Unicorn	20
The Lady-in-waiting Speaks	22
The Last Shirt of King Charles the First	24
The Female Factory	25
The Radium Girls	27
The Royal Exhibition Building	28
Louisa	30
The Loch Ard Peacock	32
The Landscape of William Buckley	34
Blossom Dreaming	36
Mr Marmalade	37
Lone Male	38
Trespasser in the Loop	39
Sunset in the City	40
Night	42
Lemon	43
Orange	44
Super Moon	45
Backyard of the Mind	46
Cape York	47
Still Life	49

Heidelberg Artists' Trail	50
Art Deco	51
The Pewter Plate	52
Explorer	54
Disappointment	55
The Dress	56
Japanese Tea Gardens	57
Uncharted	58
Geraniums	59
The African Fig	60
Seed	62
A Punt on the Lake	63
Red Sea	64
The Rhine	66
Couplets	67
Cool Change	69
Afterwards	70
Last Flight	71
The Vanished	73
The Spare Bike	74
Missing	75
Remembrance Day at the Shopping Centre	76
The Cu Chi Tunnels	78
The Killing Fields of Cambodia	79
9/11 Memorial	80
Stolpersteine	81
Tide of Flowers	83
Zion National Park, USA	84
Agility	85
Anaesthesia	87
Scare	88
Confessional	90

Notre Dame	91
Cold Turkey	92
Osprey	93
Crow	94
Next Door's Cat	95
A Cat and Two Crows	96
Waiting	97
Murmuration	98
Flight of the Homeless	100
Currawongs	101
Feeding	102
Mosquito	104
Silverfish	105
Caviar Spoon	106
Kangaroo Journey	107
The Meadows	109
Burrows	111
Detachment	112
Apocalypse	113
The Wheelbarrow	114
Swan Song	115

On the Brink

Russet and green
Sun and rain
Like so many autumn days
this one is on the brink

Somewhere celestial
the weather god is panning
for gold, dribbling water down
on mortals

A scatter of gold escapes
to rim the clouds

Should I open my umbrella
and if I do, will the wind
teasing the trees
blow it inside out

Research into ladybird wings
may make my umbrella stronger
Someone is always on the brink
of discovery somewhere

It's just a matter of a few grains
of gold in the right place

Creation

After *Nest*, a sculpture by Enver Camdal and Helen Bodycomb (1997)

Are these your ideas disguised
in a trio of quails' eggs
or maybe the eggs of Rhea or Roc

nubs of new poems nurtured
in nourishing broth
to gestate and flourish

to burst forth in triplicate
the three muses cheering
their glorious renditions

or lie dormant forever
roughened and resting
in fossilised fantasy

Waiting for the Muse

Time hangs like an anchor
on an old three-master
wallowing in waves

My every thought evaporates
or crumbles at my feet
I sweep and scrub the floor

hang out the sheets in the shadow
of rain-strewn trees. Zero chance
they'll be dry by sundown

I eat a scratch lunch of bread and fruit
and almost finish the crossword
What's a word for *vacant*?

Someone phones confirming
an appointment to fritter
more time away

Then off to the Yarra Trail
My body tires, my senses swell
to welcome wattle and currawong

At last I'm aloft
an untethered balloon
in a scurry of cloud

Poetry Pond

The poetry pond is broad and bottomless
the black glassy surface enticing poets
to its edge and holding them in thrall

Sometimes I cast a bright fly into the waters
hoping to catch a sonnet or a couplet of free verse
A wriggling worm may be bait enough

for villanelle, sestina or pantoum
and my trawling net once uncovered
an ancient limerick

Sometimes I throw a stone
watch the ripples spread and fade
like rhymes in harmony of motion

On hot days I swim the cool waters, trailing
my hands among silver snippets of stanzas
crafting a collage of slippery emotions

Floating in a welter of words
thoughts drifting from clouds to pondweed
in search of the perfect coda

Blown Away

The top of her head lifts off
to the violin concerto he renders
restless from his dreaming

Red, yellow and blue notes
splotch alphabets curling
around subterranean gloom

His eye is a target for narrative arrows
His overalls throttle her
to ecstasies of rhyme

A ladder raising the roof leads
to a shambolic forest where creeping
opinions invade a red think tank

A lone publisher under a white sky
fossicks for lyric gems hidden
in leaf litter

Memory Quilt

I stitch the quilt of my life
one piece a year

Some squares vivid with possums
sunflowers and fireflies
are firmly fixed to the whole

These symbolise joyous times
when achievement, satisfaction
and love flourished

Memories of graduation, marriage
childbirth and all those holidays
that refurbished the soul

But grief is one half of memory
and possibly more

So many squares of dark fabric
with wispy tracings
hang on by loose threads

My callused fingers worry these threads
in the hope that the squares will drop
and vanish amongst the detritus

Some squares are transparent
with the grief I have forgotten

I grieve for the absence of grief
where grief is expected to be

The Family Tree

could have been the apple
creeping with codlin and buffeted by cricket balls
or maybe the tree whose purplish flowers
I rolled between wet palms to wash them clean
or perhaps the kapok
its sleek pear-shaped fruit chock- full of silky fibres
but of course I'm only teasing

These days when all my friends are worshipping
their ancestors with only a curt bow
to their descendants
the Family Tree spreads its boughs across the lawn
dropping twigs and leaves with alarming frequency
father   mother   brother   son

The roots delve deep
and it's way down there with Pluto
that I find Mitochondrial Eve
the Seven Mothers and Mungo Man

I picture him strolling the shores of Lake Mungo
a shivering of ice smoothing the ripples
Tall and fine-boned he pauses on a sandy lunette
to spear a cavorting fish
Giant kangaroos and wombats haunt the forest

In death he is covered with red ochre
to keep his ghost at bay

Seven Mothers

All Europeans are descended from seven Stone Age women – research report

Tara, fingers stiff to breaking
gouges Tuscan soil for roots and seeds
buried beneath the ochre sheen

Syrian Jasmine ties sinews to skins
for shelter from the sirocco
Deft fingers put seeds to bed

Ursula scours the rocky Greek terrain
uses finger speech to calm
Neanderthal neighbours

On a steep Caucasian slope, Xenia
binds her hands with fur against the cold
Her fingers are signposts pointing
east and west to America

Katrine follows the glacier's retreat
north from Venice to the Alps
strokes the animals returning from exile
dips her fingers in the meltwater

Helena, working the marshy deltas
near the Franco-Spanish border
prises open rippled shells
Oysters slip with silken speed to basket
and sometimes down her throat

Velda, fingers dancing the tarantella
steals her neighbour's food
flees north from Spain to the lands
where reindeer grow velvet

Now Velda's daughter
many generations grand
eyes the microscope and teases
history from the powerhouse
in the cell's jellied broth

The Iceman

c. 3300 BCE, Otztal Alps, Italy

*Copper Age man, his skin a coppery colour
has been mummified and frozen in a glacier*

*

He sets out on a journey to find more food
than he has stolen from his neighbour
A stab wound in his small soft hand
avenges his subterfuge

Always walking, walking
his eyes oscillating
at every twitch of bush
or rustle in the rimed grass

He rests awhile, presses
his injured hand to his forehead
sees velvet green foliage
with purple edges illuminated
by the dawn

Face and arms burnt by snow and sun
his long hair protecting his shoulders
he slogs up hills and down into valleys
his snake-like path following the curve
of the hills

The air is crisp and astringent
as the lime seeds
he crunches between his teeth
He pulls his cloak closer
then creeps up to strangle
weasels and rabbits

His breath hangs like icicles
in the freezing air
He looks back and sees a figure skulking
from one tree trunk to another
He hasn't the strength to draw back a bow
heavy enough to fell a man

His pursuer, the irate neighbour
has such strength

The flint arrowhead lodges
just below his shoulder
He falls to his knees as the blood
pouring from the new wound
congeals on the icy ground

Pine trees whisper to ferns
messages spiralling like whirlwinds
He has paid for his folly
The hunter has become the prey
and the coldest of all cold cases
has been solved

The Lady and the Unicorn

After the six mediaeval tapestries hanging in the Musée National du Moyen Age, Paris

1

Still as the stitched air
I sit like a stuffed partridge
as my father sketches his next tapestry

My maid places jewels from my mother's casket
on a silk scarf around my neck
the long weight of a long line of ancestors
I must wear

The lion paws the tent flap
lashes his tongue, an open-mouth grin
The unicorn tilts his long sharp horn
towards me

Must I always submit to the passions of others
While my father stitches rabbits, goats and ducks
into fields of spring flowers, the trees will splash their fruit
and I will be stitched in with wool and wire

as surely as the tent is roped to the family tree
My flesh cut by the clothes I wear
only my maid understands me

2

Enough of this pussyfooting around
lion and unicorn pensively holding
family banners and tent flaps
while I fuss over the necklace from the casket
offered by my demure lady-in-waiting

So it's all about a sixth sense
of understanding is it
and an inner creative power
which I'm about to exert
by luring the monkey to my shoulder

harnessing together lion and unicorn
those old sparring partners
both fleet of foot
and riding off through orange groves
of a thousand flowers

Rabbits and goats bolt from my path
fabulous birds wheel overhead

Grasping the luxuriant mane
and the plunging horn
I'm no longer stitched down
but galloping through the five senses
until I reach satiety

The Lady-in-waiting Speaks

A piece of cloth from a skirt worn by Elizabeth I has been found hanging on a wall in the 13th century church of St Faith, Bacton, Herefordshire

Each time I dress my Tudor Queen
in this skirt of cobalt and crimson
lavish with gold and silver thread
I am part of this great country's destiny

On the day the Spanish Armada reared
above the skyline jostling and
bucking like spume-flecked horses
the queen wore the skirt

Her hands, wet with sweat as if she manned
the cannon, smoothed the skirt
in agitation and I touched the stains
when undressing her that night

At the execution of Mary Queen of Scots
my queen was inconsolable
tears coursing down her face
and pooling in her skirt

I tried so hard to dislodge the salt
but the colour of the cloth
changed to a pallor matched
only by my lady's skin

The queen has given me her well-worn skirt
which I hold to my heart and sew
with butterflies, frogs and squirrels
Cut and edged, it makes a splendid covering

for the altar
where my mistress kneels
begging forgiveness for all those lives
she destroyed during her glorious reign

The Last Shirt of King Charles the First

The white shirt is embroidered
the long sleeves ruffled
and edged with lace

I feel the warm worsted
stroke my arms
console my leaping heart

prevent the shivering
my audience would blame on fear
rather than the chill January air

Faces eager for blood
and spectacle gaze upward
pitiless, unforgiving

But surely there is nothing to forgive
Mine is the Divine Right of Kings
as fitting as this noble shirt

which suddenly feels flimsy
A cold breeze plays
over my collarbones

where the neckline gapes

The Female Factory

In the darkness hiding us from
the desperate men of Hobart Town
we tramp the weary miles
from Sullivan's Cove to the gaol
our legs like jelly after months at sea

and our stomachs as unpredictable
as our futures
Tin tickets on strings around our necks
dance from side to side
belying our weariness and dread

Our heads are shaved roughly
to belittle and humiliate
I lose my beautiful chestnut mane
(which has never been cut before)
to be made into wigs and sold to rich ladies

It's always cold and damp here
in the shade of Mount Wellington
and the nearby rivulet often floods
Sometimes we wade in icy water
up to our knees

My job is to pick the good fibres
out of old tarred rope for caulking ships
like the one which brought us here
Stale bread and thin soup leave me
hungry and too tired to work

As punishment in solitary
I wear the iron collar with spokes
sticking out all way round
Sleep is impossible
so the vicious cycle continues

Some are lucky enough to be sent
into service   some unlucky
enough to fall pregnant
the baby placed in the gaol nursery
where the sheets are black with fleas

Forbidden to talk we sing hymns
and folksongs to each other
scrubbing and wringing the clothes
our arms red to the elbows
as we wait for sweet release

The Radium Girls

These factory girls flirted with life
tossing their curls
flaunting their figures
hitching their skirts

and most of all painting
their faces, teeth and fingernails
with the luminous paint they used
for the dials of watches

Quite harmless
said foreman and chemist
as they donned lead aprons
So the girls being good girls

and always obeying their bosses
licked the brushes to fine points
to paint all the hours of the day
and imbibed the deadly radium

Their lives grew shorter by the minute
Time their livelihood, time their undoing
As one sickened, another took her place
Their friends were told they died of syphilis

The Royal Exhibition Building

Melbourne, November, 1959

Row upon row of desks stretching
into a lesson on perspective
Too many to count
Covered in exam papers

like white table cloths or sheets
I approach this sacrificial feast with no appetite
a stone in the stomach, and the shivery reminder
that this building was once a fever hospital

Looking for my number, the number which may appear
later in lists of success if I have the courage
to walk down the aisles to the right desk whose legs
are wadded with blotter to silence rattles

A sense of optimism, fatalism has dragged us
from suburbs at all points to the slow tram
up Bourke, screech and clatter
around the corner to Spring then Nicholson

Candidates mass like delegates to Federation but less
flamboyant, features delineated sharply on white faces
All classmates in sober school uniform except one
the beautiful one

in green and white sheath
her wavy blonde hair bouncing
on her shoulders
She fails, of course.

After three hours endurance
a tentative blossoming
rosy cheeks, a waving of palms
The building prepares for the next show

Louisa

Louisa Barrow was the partner of Sir Redmond Barry for thirty-four years and the mother of his four children

In the small Fitzroy house
that Redmond bought me
I am kneading the dough
pummelling and thwacking
down hard on the floured board
then gently moulding

I have mixed in sugar and salt
rather like Redmond's changeable
moods and wait for the rising
and the baking of the bread
to be eaten with a slathering
of love for our supper

The twelve-bottle spice set ranged
along the counter mimics the jury
in the Supreme Court
where Redmond is judge
Some fiery, some bland but all distinctly
different and suited to the purpose

As patron of the Melbourne Public Library-
in-waiting he lends his own books to jurors
I, too have borrowed some cookbooks
for the fine drawings of pheasants, farms
and colonial geese but stumble over
ingredients and new ways of doing things

Tomorrow I will hang
a hare in the pantry
and the washing on the line
while Redmond decides the fate
of that outlaw who is wont
to wear a saucepan on his head

The Loch Ard Peacock

The *Loch Ard* was wrecked near Port Campbell on 1 June 1878 with the loss of most lives. A Minton porcelain peacock was undamaged.

The sea is a peacock
strutting its plumage
head bobbing back and forth

turquoise shallow water
feathering into the royal blue
of the deep

Dark whirlpools
the eyes on the tail
ambush the ship's hull

Waves slam cliffs
then sag until energised
by irrevocable rhythm

Fingers of rock, webbing
worn away over aeons
thrust towards me

Bones of the shipwrecked
fuse with ancestral shells
in the striped limestone

Now wind hurls foam
and like an enraged bird
it blinds me for a moment

The ship jolts and shudders
Women shriek
like a muster of peacocks

I hold fast
as barnacle to spar
The ship founders

Gasping, blue with cold
the cabin boy grips my hair
steers me to shore

We cling together
exhausted
on the only beach for miles

Beside us
head buried in the sand
the porcelain peacock

The Landscape of William Buckley

Point Lonsdale, Victoria

Escaping the soldiers
and the men transported with him
Buckley wound his tall frame
like a clock spring

into the sandstone cave snagging
his clothes on the jagged opening
He knocked shellfish against the rocks
releasing the sweet salty flesh

seized for a walking stick
a spear marking a grave
and was welcomed into the tribe
as the dead man's spirit

For thirty-two years he shared the food
of the Wathaurung, laboured
with them, learned their language
to sooth blood feuds

Now red blush of saltbush
surrounds the lighthouse
above Buckley's cave
barred in steel against the curious

The old Norfolk pine twinkles
its lights to wreck-strewn reefs
Beyond the breakers, humpback
whales sport their flukes

The intemperate coastline
softens to tidal flats
where spoonbills fossick
like fastidious great-aunts

Blossom Dreaming

I'm lying on the ground looking up
The sky passes through all hues
of blue as twilight descends

Each leaf becomes a cherry blossom
then turns to cotton wool
and my thoughts to marshmallow

The statue in flickering shadow
waves her arms wildly
trying to distort my state of mind

Somewhere in the distance
a train's horn penetrates fog
A dog barks at the last shreds of light

I walk through avenues of petals
So much softness underfoot
so much glorious waste for fruit to ripen

I ponder the paints and perfumes
of women focused on the same purpose
as darkness obliterates the lot

Mr Marmalade

On a summer's night in the city
an eerie purple light
spangles the interlaced canopies
of trees

A breeze teases fallen leaves
into a scurry
Stars work their magic as people
hurry from dinner to show

Trams, each with the weight
of fourteen rhinos
commandeer the street
sardining cars into narrow lanes
on either side

As we sit in the tram shelter
a young man in orange suit
and bowler hat materialises
shuffling a deck of cards
Pick a card, any card

The travellers beside us
lift their eyes from their mobiles
catching the lilt of the magic
their faces transformed

Lone Male

Sometimes I see one
a lost look on his face
shuffling along an aisle
in the supermarket
peering at labels

He may ask a housewife
for advice or phone home
for weights and brands
the confidence of office or clinic
having deserted him

If left to his own devices
his basket will hold sausages
white bread, cola and crisps
his plight obvious
to the casual eye

How much happier he is
as hunter than gatherer

Trespasser in the Loop

A cold wind signals the train's approach
Sad scraps of paper flap between rails
People emerge clutching coats around them

I clamber aboard to the soothing voice
affirming the train's destination
The blue wall panels glide backwards

In the panther-black tunnel
a thud on the carriage roof
and feet padding back and forth

All passengers must disembark at the next station
A trespasser in the loop has left a package…
so the rumour runs feasting and fattening on fear

Passengers jab at mobile phones
a ticket inspector crosses himself
and a guitarist plays 'Nearer my God to Thee'

A glistening cobweb reflects small packets of light
to dispel the gloom and sends small packets
of sound to locate the prey

Near the exit in a patch of weak light
a clump of violets struggles to survive
the violence brewing below

Sunset in the City

The western sky is mango cream
watermelon-glazed
finished with chocolate tracery

Down below, the hungry and homeless
keep their eyes on the ground watching
fairy lights reflected in puddles

Sell me a cigarette pleads a woman
to a huddle of boisterous young men
who eye her voraciously

Didgeridoos drown out conversation
a blind man in a wheelchair croons
country and western songs

his rich baritone fit for the stage
and an old woman sings of past loves
not caring if anyone listens

Too late for shopping
too early for raging
malaise envelops the streets

In the station, seagulls shriek
at the timorous or disabled amongst them
as they scour for titbits

On the train, a much-travelled young man
sleepy beyond endurance, asks passengers
one by one, to wake him at Greensborough

All shake their heads mumbling disapproval
as he sinks into slumber and is carried
to the end of the line

Night

Night folds its wings
over a clutch of sunset colours
Most birds have roosted
Only the owls are alert

wingbeats soft, round eyes
pools of moving shadows
ears tuned to the rustles
and squeaks only they can hear

Love flickers like a night light
quickly extinguished
Bottles are drained of bravado
to challenge the dark

Shoots sprout just as children
grow in their sleep
Lemons hang like miniature moons
from topmost branches inaccessible

even to rakes
It's impossible to tell if the sky is cloudy
or a faintly illuminated shade of black
rather the way our minds behave

when faced with intractable problems

Lemon

The lemon tree flourishes
though stunted by savage pruning
that stripped back fifty years of galls

No more thrips, cosy and hungry
to sap the sugar stream
ideally producing large juicy lemons
instead of small green apologies

I'd known, many lemons ago
that surgery was the answer
but like a human weighing
the pros and cons of an operation
I'd dithered until the gardener
firmly planted his foot

Now pink-tinged leaves curl saucily
and buds bejewel the boughs
The dwarf tree stands rejuvenated

Orange

Late on a cold night
I crave an orange
It sits in the centre of the bowl
and my whole world revolves around it

I peel the thin skin
discard the pith before
it bites into my quicks
divide the fruit into segments
then suck out the goodness
sweet juice flooding my senses

Above the ash tree the moon
not wanting to be eclipsed
masquerades as a lemon
Its yellow light lassoes a winter iris
and casts a sour beam on the vine
burgeoning and strangling by stealth
shrubs and trees alike

Super Moon

Look east toward the ocean
and just where it flirts with the sky
you should see, with any luck
the super moon rising

Full moon at perigee*
larger and more lustrous
than you've ever seen
or are likely to see

A mystery since ancient time
we feel we own the moon
and since Apollo landed
have had a stake in it

We peer from the front garden
we peer from the back
branches plucking our sleeves
but see nothing except street lights

No orange ball of Edam cheese
No Mad Hatter's tea party
where seas meet craters
Sky overcast and gloomy as a jilted bride

A tide of regret from would-be moon gazers
joins with king tides around the world
and an octopus washes into
a Florida garage

* The point in the moon's orbit that is closest to the earth

Backyard of the Mind

Mulched autumn leaves peppered
with pollen. Consider the mellow
thoughts which spring from this soil

Worms tunnel through turbulent
topography, snails slick slime
on rough edges of theories

A creeper of unknown origin
winds like white matter through grey
its tendrils curling question marks

Berries proliferate like blood blisters
on meninges and when squashed
cause slippage and the turning of ankles

Lemons tart as rumours begin
and beguile as sweet-smelling flowers
fruit green then yellow with age

The rose climbing the eucalypt
adds romance to the mix wafting
petals to perfume skulduggery

The pine tree drops needles
to repair torn images
and cones to startle the reflexes

One blink and you miss
this hotbed of creativity

Cape York

The oldest rocks in the world
eroded to red dust daubing
cars, clothes and consciousness

Green tangle of rainforest where lawyer
vines pluck sleeves compelling
us to consider our choices

At night cassowary plums bounce
off the roof of our cabin
a pelting tired bodies could do without

Termite mounds point north-south
encompassing silence
Inside the scurry never ceases

Wallabies, brumbies and
the odd wild boar flash
and fade between grasstrees

A python winds itself like a corkscrew
down a coconut palm as we follow
blue butterflies to an even bluer sea

Oceans of beaches with wide white sands
at the mercy of crocodiles submerged
amongst hooped mangrove roots

Some say the sacrificial leaves
of the mangrove
collect salt for the whole tree

turn yellow and die
but we who are less altruistic
clamber over rocks to the very tip

of the continent, dip our toes
in the sea and wave for photos
with the world at our backs

Still Life

I'm standing at the window
on a grey autumn day

No breath of wind rustles
rosebush or melaleuca
Even clouds prop
above the confettied lawn

A kookaburra wipes its beak on the fence
and pears simmer on the stove
A toy apple dangles spindly legs
with cherry feet over the window ledge

The flour jar shaped like a pot-bellied bear
grins companionably at the china frog
swallowing the scouring pad
The fridge hums background music

On the wall hangs a painting of pheasant
grapes, quiche and a tankard of frothing beer
all in muted tones as are mine
when I tell you what's for dinner

Nothing as sumptuous as the painted feast
but that fare is cold, hard and remote
whereas I've turned on the oven
and appetising smells are wafting from it

to mingle with your special scent
as I fold you in my arms

Heidelberg Artists' Trail

A dog hauling on its leash
noses the base of a shattered gum
A cyclist careers past, tossing up gravel
to arc through *plein-air*

On the Yarra bank, the houses
absent a century ago, ghost in and out
Horses nibble sweet grass
with the same devotion to detail as then

Streeton sits in his eyrie
sketches a distant eagle
hovering over the river
His palette is awash with blues

greens and a touch of gold for the sun
about to slip behind cloud
He licks his brush to a point
mixes red with blue for the purpling

that deepens as the sun descends
No roar of traffic, just the murmur
of bees in the blossom and the trickling
of water over stones

Art Deco

Hats hugging heads
Dresses striped, sparkling, tiered

strokeable, flowing from high waist
or shoulder, skimming knees

Remembered from childhood days
dressing up in mother's ball gowns

Viewers flow too, in orderly slow-step
biting off small portions of chat

some pithy, some trite
eyes darting between morsels of memory

Caught in silver gelatine
celebrities and hoi polloi

A mannequin in sleek one-piece
poised over a shimmering 'pool'

We glide past the water wall
enchantment for small hands

and out to the boulevard
trees spangled with fairy lights

The Pewter Plate

Nailed to a post on Dirk Hartog Island off the coast of Western Australia by William de Vlamingh in 1697

This place of sand dunes and saltbush
safe harbour for our square rigger
welcomes us with a wealth of seafood
Mackerel flaunt their iridescence
minnows streak rock pools

In amongst rainbow coral I snare a turtle
which when separated from its carapace
and boiled over a campfire
makes delicious soup
slurped from a pewter bowl

With a rock I pound the bulbs of red lilies
in my bowl, mortar and pestle style
and feel wise as an apothecary
Heaven knows, we need something
to heal our bleeding gums

On the second day, a cyclone
fierce enough to drive sand grains
into pewter, batters the camp
The chain anchoring our boat clanks
like ghostly shackles

Soon after the blinding turbulence
I hammer the bowl into a plate
inscribe it with my name and Hartog's
nail it to a pine post
and leave this benighted island

Explorer

After the paintings of Albert Tucker

In black loneliness, he stands like a god
his legs wide apart
supporting a fretwork trunk
his head a two-edged hatchet

He is one in a pantheon
forged out of a dreamtime
a necessary makeshift
for Olympus and Troy

His face weathered rock
his coat rough eucalypt bark
and under his scarified skin
his veins trace a lattice of vines

Hero, chasing a river to water strange crops
felling forests for alien herds
or destroyer of a fragile wilderness
where hooves crush remnant soil

and native fauna cower in ever deeper burrows
Or, no archetype, he confronts
the desert within and knows it will win
no matter how long the sortie

Vengeful parrots, all beaks and claws
arrow past his head

Disappointment

They climbed the mount
as far as their frail knees would carry them
but the summit was shrouded in cloud
The lake they skirted was brackish
meandering into nothingness
On rounding the cape the only island
bristled with thistles

The old explorers had their fill
of disappointment as if looking
down the wrong end of a telescope

In suburbia it's becoming the norm

You're late for an appointment
because the train is delayed
the storm cuts your power and severs
a limb of a favourite tree
a meeting is cancelled
a new chef ruins the dinner

So many balloons buoyant
and beautiful punctured at once

Trying to float while drowning
in despond you remember
a smile
a welcome cup of coffee
a new rose awakening
a door held open

The Dress

The dress in soft blue-grey wool
painstakingly sewn by my mother
clung to my teenage curves

She teamed it with a wine-red
cardigan she had knitted
adding a strand of heirloom pearls

We paraded her handiwork
and my fragile self-esteem
in front of my father

who said:
Stand up straight
Shoulders back

Japanese Tea Gardens

San Francisco

Far from the razzamatazz of Fisherman's Wharf
and tourists spilling from cable trams
A whistle stop on the Red Bus tour
where the Golden Gate hangs in the mist

Despite people thronging
around pagodas and stone lanterns
stepping up and over the drum bridge
a stillness overarches these gardens

A heron stands, a statue of itself
in a clear stream watching
golden carp nuzzle the bottom
Cherry trees blossom in the Zen grove

My eyes record a flush of red and orange
on a backdrop of startling green
Other cameras are wanting
in this harmony of colour and light

We who have just stepped off
a long-haul flight
need such sustenance
for souls battered by life

Uncharted

After *Lost and Found* by Amanda Peluso 2017, Giclee print on archival paper

Shards of emerald descend a sunbeam
My hands open to catch them
Other hands join in from pink spheres

rolling gently
through the undergrowth
and rising into the sky

Until now, no-one has set foot in this forest
with their no-nonsense hiking boots
to crush the new fronds, furry and unfurling

No one has trapped a butterfly
or squashed an iridescent beetle
No licence to kill exists here

Raindrops mingling with tears
sprinkle a baptism of sorts
Tracks spiral and twist

beckoning, tantalising
There are no signposts but I know
it doesn't matter which way I go

Geraniums

Opening my door into autumn
I see geraniums, aflame
and defiant, umbrella flowers
over velvety leaves

Tough as army biscuits
(though eaten by larvae of the mouse moth)
they bloom from tropics to tundra
from sand to clay

Never seen in florist shops or hobnobbing
with roses and orange blossom at weddings
relegated to the lowest class of flora
they flourish in pots on student balconies

or in the window boxes of Europe
nurtured with patriotic passion
Poor cousin to the red poppy of Flanders
each flower has ten stamens and five carpels

tipped with a long glabrous awn
(Lewis Carroll-speak for a slender
seed-bearing bristle)
resembling a crane's bill

You may never have known this
but it gives geraniums a Zen quality
elevating them in floral lore
and justifying this poem

The African Fig

New leaves, pinkly green, peep
over the windowsill, enticing me
into the chilly Melbourne dawn

For the first time in thirty years
twin figs, plump and purple
cling to the creeper which in turn
grim-fastens to brick

Where it revels in sunlight
above the balcony
its leaves are twine-veined
and several old larger
than those below

Surviving drought, repair men
and window cleaners ripping away
the fragile glue, it bows
under its own weight
heavy as figgy pudding

New stems make their points
Leaves hosting an occasional spider
are not harried here
by the antelope's hot snuffle

The womb-shaped fig bursting
with seed joins us in fruitfulness
but this foreign plant is not welcome
in our country

has no right to survive and thrive
An unwanted refugee to be uprooted
and discarded like the weeping willow

Seed

Pity the seed its odyssey
by land, water and sky

naked to clashes
with bully or devourer

given the brushoff by insects
searching for sweetness

deep in petalled dresses
lustrous and alluring

days of patience
to reach fruition

dispatched by parachute
to land on barren ground

lost in the labyrinthine guts
of greedy birds

hitching a ride on shaggy coats
So much lost potential

Pity the seed its blind gamble
on a fragile future

A Punt on the Lake

Cocooned from the storm and stress
of traffic the lake basks
in stippled light under a grey sky

The boatman gently plies his pole
manoeuvring our craft
away from chattering strollers

On a backdrop of pampas fronds
giant lily leaves frame water
coloured a furtive green by algae

At the edge of a forested island
a male swan sits upright on the nest
while his mate enjoys a leisurely lunch

A quartet of cormorants
waits for fish
to come within beaks' reach

Canna lilies drip blood
on to the green palette
where coot walk on water

No sign of rats or foxes
to muddy the midday scene
A bellbird chimes a cascade

of
joyous
notes

Red Sea

Swimming in blood I tongue the words
rich for the tapestry of world history,
rusty for that taste we all know
so redolent of iron:
swords guns bullets bombs

I strike out strongly
towards a shore I cannot see
keeping my head above water
breathing deeply

then dive below the surface
to hear the sounds of death
to scan all those wars
fading into shadow
since man evolved

Never has there been a time
without war ravaging
people and landscape
blood soaking the earth
running in rivers

War swims through the currents
of blood, thickening its substance
pulling me down to tangle
with the strongest seaweed
holding fast to rock

Oysters and scallops dwelling
in the murk have neither blood
nor tongue and cannot swim
for their lives yet somehow
they give hope of peace

The Rhine

Barges full of sand and mystery
plough the Rhine
past pylons of old bridges
bombed into forgetfulness

Our boat glides over pewter furrows
to wait imprisoned in the dark lock
Water rising notch by notch
steps us upriver

Vineyards in serried rows
slope to ruined castles
where barons lurked to rob small craft
or lock the crews in island dungeons

Shorn of their gold, many succumbed
to the honeyed song of the Lorelei
combing her golden hair
on the shipwrecking rocks

Couplets

Battened down in the cool understory
all windows closed

all curtains drawn
against the threat of a scorching day

Under the eaves
a soft scratch on the trunk

of a dying tree fern
two magpies, parent and young

pant like dogs and peck the soil
for a dribble of water from the hose

When I open the door, one decamps
while the other props defiantly

Two baby possums
commas in the tale

fall to their death
in a stroke of heat

In the Gippsland bush, two kangaroos
mother with joey in pouch huddle

beside the only eucalypt not burning
as if waiting for Noah

Embers fanned by a vicious north wind
torch everything they touch

Down at the stricken river
two fish amongst a million dead

swim in desultory fashion
Not enough water to douse a fire

or to keep the fish alive
Fins undulate at an ever slower pace

Light reflects in a rainbow arc
from a billion scales

Cool Change

A nuance in the air as it trips the light
Birds sense it before we do
and announce it with disturbed chirping

We know the wind has turned
in a blustering arc as leaves pirouette
down the path and branches fence

with one another
Temperature slides down the bannister
curtains dance through up-flung windows

and even the most house-proud forgives
the dust riding the currents
Flushed faces welcome the saviour of sanity

Afterwards

A Walk in the Fog and Snow, Kinglake, 10 June 2009, Lloyd Godman, 2009, pigment print on archival paper

Smoke no longer veils the sun
It is now winter's turn

Snow has smoothed trampled ground
covered soft flakes of ash

cooled boiling sap
and bubbling bark

Trees seared into memory
mark exclamations on a white page

fingers pointing
backs bending

Footprints stop at the cross
uprooted, cast aside

Last Flight

He has filled in his departure card
removed and replaced his shoes
tossed a full water bottle into the garbage
been shot with air bullets to check for drugs

battled boredom with a stoicism
borne of repetition
and is finally seated, luggage stowed
in the protective mother bird

His fear of flying is quelled
by the sight of cottonwool clouds
He has always been just ahead
or just behind disaster

Blinds not yet drawn on darkness
he sees his reflection with a frisson
of alarm and wonders if the worst
should happen would he

white and rigid with fear
gabble of love and hope
in his essential solitude
or descend into despair

Somewhere on the ocean
a fisherman sees lights
spiralling down and thinks
of shooting stars

Friends pick up the tangled ball of grief
to unravel it back to the source
while we, having flown the same plane
just days before

ponder what makes us
more worthy than the missing
and thank God, fate or a galaxy
of lucky stars for our survival

The Vanished

Once it's gone and something fills the gap
you can't remember what was there before
Regret and recall both have left the map

A tooth well-rotted cracks with just a tap
You plan on dentures, implants, crowns and more
Once it's gone then something fills the gap

Want coffee, bread or maybe ginger snaps
Can't find what used to be your favourite store
Regret and recall soon will leave the map

What happened to that gumtree, laced with blackened sap
No hint of trunk or branches: you really can't be sure
once it's gone and something fills the gap

Friends may die through many a cruel mishap
For years the pangs of loss disturb your core
until regret and recall leave the map

Though you're alert and you've no handicap
the blessing of forgetting heals the sore
Once they're gone and someone fills the gap
regret and recall both will leave the map

The Spare Bike

The front wheel nudges a loose-rolled hose
resting on scuffed bricks
Both tyres slim but flat
handlebars curled like rams' horns

the faded red and yellow frame stripped
of all adornment for the race of our son's life
back arched like a gazelle, muscles pumping
No mudguards or lights to slow this road runner

Tendrils of unstoppable creeper breach
the join between shed roof and wall
gleam whitely in pale light
weave around spokes

A spinning spider nests under the seat
egg sacs bulging
So the cycle continues, waiting for the ghost
rider in bright lycra to spin the wheels

Missing

I'm standing on a wintry platform
Two seagulls tussle for a crust
Trains rattle and roll

On a nearby pillar, ads cycle
enticing passengers to try a red wine
surpassing a lover's caress

or buy the fast car that dissolves
and reforms into a cheetah
chasing its prey

Between the car and the wine
the image of a young girl's face
stops and stares rebelliously

School uniform, braided hair
pale complexion and
missing for a year

Caught between the wine and the car
by a man who offered her both
she may be dead or desolate

or just too busy with life
to phone the ones
who gave life to her

Remembrance Day at the Shopping Centre

11/11/2011, 11 a.m.

An auspicious day
occurring once a century
a day to remember
the memories of all
previous remembrance days
War and peace playing
stacks-on-the-mill

The mall manager announces
a minute's silence
Customers stop arguing
the price of fish or bananas
small boys pause
their video wars
the rat-a-tat of crockery
dwindles to a tinkle
the troop-train shriek
of coffee machines
dies to a gentle puff

Three jets in blue brilliance
fly over and back

People stand still
or move in slow motion
thinking, if briefly
of death and destruction
Trigger fingers relax
on handbags and trolleys
until the reveille sounds
and old habits march on

The Cu Chi Tunnels

South Vietnam

I stop running
lean into ballooning exhaustion
lift the trapdoor camouflaged
with stressed leaves then
edge along the narrow entrance

Artillery thunders and echoes
through ravaged jungle
roped above my head

Fearful of the gloom
my eyes grab every chink of light
My gut clenches

I flatten against the soft earth wall
my heart a tumult of complaint
then glide like a wisp of smoke
from the cooking fire

forgetting for the moment
scorpions, runaway malaria
and the shock of the close shave

The Killing Fields of Cambodia

Bamboo encircles this ragged plot
each pole decorated with a bracelet
in rainbow colours

After decades ravaged
by insect and worm, bones
buried in suffocating soil

move accusingly to the surface
to be harvested and sequestered
in a many-tiered monument

Children were grabbed by the ankles
skulls smashed against the Cannonball tree
or throats cut with razor-edged palm fronds

Many still lived when buried
their thin cries drowned out
by loudspeakers hanging from branches

Tourists try but fail
to understand
Birds and cicadas fall silent

9/11 Memorial

I have ridden the subway to the end of the line
and emerge into ebullient Wall Street
I head straight for two square pools
set in grey stone marking the footprints
of The World Trade Centre

Inscribed in black around the edges
are the names of workers
visitors and first responders
whose lives were taken
An unborn child is nameless

White roses mark the birthdays
of the dead

Water, quiet at the top of each pool
cascades over the edges of inner squares
and vanishes into some deep well

A man sleeps rough on the steps
of a nearby church and a huge
white bird spreads stone wings
over the crowd

Stolpersteine

(Stumbling Stones)

The hobnailed boots of orange sellers
pound the cobble-stones
outside Bertha's house

The carriage wheels of bakers
add to the daily grind

Later, jackboots beat out
a rhythm on the stones as Bertha
and her family are driven
to the cattle trucks

Always a grinding
a wearing down
like the sharpening of knives

At the camp she hears
the shuffling of feet
mostly one-way

sees the piles of shoes
new/old/black/brown
and one small pair

red patent leather
with a daisy buckle

And now, huddling amongst
the cobblestones, a concrete block
topped with a brass plaque

engraved *Here lived Bertha…*
one of many placed from Germany
to Russia to Spain

Soft-soled shoes polish and caress
the plaques into memory

Tide of Flowers

Yesterday, storm waters surged across the garden
sluicing rose petals through the garage
Soil washed from beds reveals
scores of bleached snail shells
their occupants long gone

On days such as these I hark back
to the collapse of ancient landscapes
torrents of rain filling the hollows
the weight of sediments fossilising shells
into memory

Sea lilies waving in currents
where eucalypt and bottlebrush now stand

Slippage along fault lines
uplift into bright skies
a folding as if a giant tossed
a rumpled cloth over the land
Infernos besting our worst bushfires

Such cataclysms, often man-made
keep happening. Some pass un-noticed
Others are marked in boulevard
and mall by a tide of flowers
cut off at the peak of their blooming

Zion National Park, USA

Rising straight up out of desert
it doesn't take my breath away

but rather quickens it
in startled admiration
for those forces
that shook a sandy beach

squashed it, weathered it
into peaks, mesas, canyons
maple red in gold
of elder and wild grape

During all those years
of lording it
over coyotes, hikers and snakes
the same forces have steadily

invisibly humbled the mountains
cutting them down to size
back to the sandy beach
of their birth

And when I die
some particle of me
borne northward on currents
of sea and air may join them

in the slow motion cycle
of boom and bust

Agility

This poem does not have legs
at least not the right kind
but each day it's working
to improve the situation

I would like it to trampoline
like a kangaroo
or bound like a cat straight up a tree

Maybe it could hurdle fences
or weave like a skateboard rider
or cut a lazy zig-zag
down a snow-flurried slope

Sometimes the poem leaves a silver trail
and I know it's progressing
ever so slowly on its stomach foot
but that's not good enough
in this fast-paced world

I want it to have legs
which could basket pollen
before flying back to the sweetness
of the hive

If I wait a few aeons
it might crawl out of its swamp
like an ancient fish
on its leglike fins

But really I think the solution
could be a hip replacement
and when at last this happens
my poem will leap from sloth
like a mountain goat

Anaesthesia

You may think I'm plunging
into a bottomless well
its sides black with slime

or taking flight
above the clouds
through a starless sky

or becalmed on a midnight sea
no other craft around, no sound
not even soft lapping

But for me on this table
no plunge, no flight, no gentle sea
no dreams, nothing

I'm out for someone's count
in this state of oblivion
which may or may not be dark

Surely theatre lights are blazing
as the surgeon unpicks my bones
unravels my gut

I surface to contusions of battle
to intrusions of the world
Liquids in, liquids out

A total loss of memory
a rekindling of the senses
as I ascend from the void

Scare

A snowstorm of mail lands on the doormat
two days after we do, back from our holiday
A letter postmarked a month ago
warns of a problem with my breast screen

...some uncertainty
...needs further investigation
Please make an appointment
at your earliest convenience

A letter postmarked a fortnight ago
...you have not responded
...matter of some urgency
...your case has been red-flagged

Imagine finding the first letter
just before leaving for Canada
Thoughts of biopsies, mastectomies
therapies creeping through my mind

reaching tumour size whenever I saw
a snow-capped mamelon
a bowl of cherries
or a deer suckling her young

I act swiftly

music smoothing an edgy wait
amongst gowned patients
with fear-flecked eyes
who come and go on slippered feet

My husband reads a magazine
without turning the pages
Then an ultrasound
and the all-clear

We float, all smiles
out to the street
where partners pace and puff
ash tumbling from glowing embers

Confessional

Pope Francis has advised hairdressers to avoid gossip conversing only in
Christian style with their clients – 'Odd Spot', *The Age*

She stroked the Black Dog of depression
brushing her client's hair from crown
to split ends

painted on the darkest dye
in her repertoire with just a few
foils for light relief

massaged the broken love affair,
oil from her fingers smoothing
the tense scalp

crimped the estranged daughter
into a manageable memory

wielded the hair dryer to warm
the omens of divorce and death

Gentle teasing into a bouffant
banished the irate husband

A lemon-scented lacquer dissolved
the drug-addicted son

Styles come and go from beehive
to mohawk and so many more
but never had she been asked
for a Christian style

Notre Dame

From stone, lead and the wood
of five thousand oaks
generations of men built this cathedral
Many fell to their deaths as their souls
soared to heaven

All who knew the flying buttresses
rose windows and immense bells
mourned as the fire rampaged

At first, white smoke as if a new pope rose
from the ashes then the black smoke
of indecision and despair sweetened
by the smell of toffeed honey
from the hives on the roof

Napoleon was crowned here
the liberation of Paris celebrated here
and in this age of scepticism
tourists have visited to confess their sins
while practising their French

Despite the crumpled spire, Notre Dame
still dwarfs the spirits of most
who have preached here

Cold Turkey

The old woman had ordered a turkey
in plenty of time for Christmas
Calling to collect
she is having regrets

When the massive bird drops
like a cannonball into her basket
she knows she'll have trouble
hauling it home

Will her fridge and oven
have room for such bulk
Should she freeze it
while biding her time

Oh no the poulterer squawks
from on high
thawing would take far too long
So stuffed with doubt she forgets

the cranberries and breadcrumbs
to fill the bird's cavity
Her children, wrapped up
in themselves urge her

to stay off the pills
They don't care if she sleeps
or not as long as their bird
makes it to the oven on time

Osprey

I'm surprised they didn't shoot the osprey
its nest a racegoer's hat
trailing flowers and ribbons
plopped on top of a light pole

Shorted the circuits once in a while
torching the stubble
riling farmers and train travellers
while the osprey lazy-winged it
back from the lake
a large fish twitching
slippery in its talons

I guess they've gone soft
recognise a fellow warrior
just trying to make ends meet
So tipping their hats at superior skills
they moved the nest to a totem pole

Crow

A crow oils
its way
into my garden
sidewalks
through winter detritus
grey-eyes me
balefully
daring me
to retrieve the twig
it has filched
to nest
the new generation
of omens

Next Door's Cat

The cure is not the wattle swanking
its gold along the river walk
or the river itself tumbling
around crippled tree trunks
but the cat, absent for weeks
like my poetic muse

Tonight I hear the soft saw
of paw on flywire

Once inside, the rearing to my hand
insinuation of grey striped body
around wooden or fleshly leg
the scrape of rough tongue on leftovers
stanzas of purrs with tail for enjambment
his curling up on the mohair rug a metaphor
for ownership and contentment

Later, in tune with some primal clock
a broad hint at the front door
a padding forth to conduct the nocturne
of possums and owls, leaving a poem
with a wistful and buoyant ending

A Cat and Two Crows

A pied cat
its raccoon tail airbrushed
stretches full length

sharpens its claws pointedly
on the wooden sleeper and leaps
to the trunk of the gum

scrambling its way
up rickety branches
to the roof

A chorus of squawks from mynahs
and magpies crescendos
over aerial acres of terracotta

Flapping their regalia as ushers
of the house, two large crows
materialise, one behind the cat

edging it back towards the spouting
the other on the high branches
pointing downwards with its beak

No pussy footing
The cat hurtles down the tree
to terra firma

to the relief of all concerned

Waiting

I'm standing at the window
watching grey clouds rumpling
the middle distance

hoping for the curtains to bell
inward with the quickening
of the southerly breeze

listening for the plink
of raindrops on the pane
for the whip crack of lightning

Suddenly my focus shifts
to a branch in the foreground
Two tawny frogmouths

camouflaged as galls
of feathery bark
keep company in silence

one asleep so it seems
the other on guard
its dark eyes fixed on mine

We three are waiting
for the next turn of events:
for the cool change

for the dark
for the time to go
searching out dinner

Murmuration

reminds me of lovers
in quiet conversation
all others excluded
from their aura

or maybe a heart murmuring
fatigue and monotony
into my unreceptive ears

Keats' 'Ode to a Nightingale'
transports me to
The murmurous haunt of flies
on summer eves

But these thoughts take on
a new shade of meaning
as they soar with thousands of birds
wheeling and swooping in a giant cloud
whose borders dissolve and reform
in response to secret codes

Leaders tire
and others replace them
the whole synchronised mass
progressing
to some predestined plan

perplexing a raptor
keeping warm
navigating to a new food source

Whatever the reason
for such glorious upheaval
I marvel at the magic
of perfect coordination
and singleness of purpose

It's only my thoughts
unable to compute
that are left in confusion

Flight of the Homeless

Just after sunrise, a noise ripples
the surface of my consciousness
and grows ever louder
Wasps, a revving truck, an aeroplane…
no, a chainsaw
bête noire of this leafy outpost

My eyes track to the house behind mine
where a eucalypt soars to fifty metres
A man in hot pink, helmet and goggles
swings ape-like on ropes
his saw severing the branch above him

spraying sawdust from ruptured vessels
Perhaps he'll fall, this pulp-board apologist
overblown with glib excuses
this destroyer of homes of hundreds
from beetle to bird

No more wind-whispers or shade
no more hide-and-seek in hollows
At sunset, flocks of currawong
displaced by bushfires, return home
for the nightly roost and chit-chat
They circle bewildered

Currawongs

Blacker than magpies
whiter than crows
the currawongs sing their sorrow
for the snow gums of the high country
where they roosted and nested
a decade ago before Black Saturday
ravaged the landscape

Their classic notes
rising above the squawks
of the mynas and the raucous jazz
of the cockatoos were once
accompanied by the soughing
of wind in the snow gums
and the whoosh of skis

Down south in the lowlands
migrants forcibly displaced
they have made their new homes
waiting another four decades
for their old haunts to welcome
them back when the snow gums
finally regenerate

Feeding

An armada of pelicans
bobbing in the slow swell
waits for its morning snack
fills beak-bags with proffered fish
rations for lean moments
Beaks softly scissors aside
cormorants diving
and weaving for scraps

Six kookaburras perch
on the red gum fence
dusk a backdrop of birdcalls
The ranger saunters along the row
feeds each the same size morsel
One bird flies from third place
to seventh and gobbles up
a second helping

Dolphins frolic at the jetty
warming up the sunset crowd
cameras clicking and flashing
As buckets of fish are planted in sand
the dolphins line up, nose to the shallows
Waves of the intrepid,
small fish in hand
advance and retreat

At next morning's breakfast
guests drawn by the nose
swarm over the buffet
piling plates with egg, fruit, toast,
eager to eat their money's worth
and a lot more besides
Some, by sleight of hand
bag an apple or muffin for lunch

Mosquito

Wrapped in a soft armchair
mohair nuzzling my knees
I'm watching my favourite program
Rain spatters the window

A possum walks over the moon
and I'm almost asleep in the dim light
when a mosquito flies
a zig-zag path across the screen

Jumping up from my stupor
I track it from carved-up corpse
to copper's blood sausage sandwich
to stagnant ditch beside the highway

Cross-eyed and vengeful
I've completely lost the plot
I finally swat the mosquito admitting
the spot of blood into evidence

An ad for fly spray splashes the screen
and the credits roll

Silverfish

Sometimes I wish
as a counterfeit fish
of silvery hue
to be transformed
into my namesake

my strong fins
scything the ripples
my body undulating
through maidenhair weed

a minnow's shadow caught
by sharp eyes
its tail devoured
by sharp teeth

But here I am in your library
groping along shelves
in the dust of my friends
inside your books
between pages of poems

holding them hostage
eating your words
hoping to read
with my sensitive feet
and digest a few lines of praise

Caviar Spoon

After *Caviar Spoon* 1995 by Simon Icarus Baigent, artwork in gold, ebony, mother of pearl, diamond, ruby

A spoon more precious
than the eggs
that fill it to the brim
made of milky mother of pearl
with diamond and ruby trim

The ebony handle
is crowned with gold
as a queen's sceptre would be
You savour the salty tang of love
from the depths of the Caspian Sea

I could give you a pendant
to circle your throat
or an emerald to nest in your hair
but have chosen a gift for exquisite taste
to have, to hold and to share

Kangaroo Journey

On a cool morning
eighteen kangaroos
range across the hill
beside the old silos
Skittish as a football team
before the final siren

Some play cat-and-mouse
some bound to vantage points
some stand tall, ears swivelling
mesmerised by passing traffic
One takes umbrage and the fence
in one bound

My husband looks up
from his breakfast paper
His eyes track movement
in the back garden
A dog perhaps, in fact
the kangaroo nibbling

a rose bush with the help
of dainty forepaws
It stares quizzically into the room
A rattling of shutters
and it's off through the jasmine
leaping the wall cleanly

to the whoops
of the children next door
Neighbours call the Wildlife Service
A shot of sedative and one more
rebellious adolescent is back
with the family

The Meadows

Translation of 'Las Vegas'

On the Strip it's hard
to imagine those meadows fed by
secret springs to green exuberance

maybe harbouring a frog, a snail
and two birds in a bush all hedging
their bets in the survival stakes

The bass beat penetrates
to the core, revving my heart
like a thwarted Ferrari

Girls in short skirts and spike heels
chatter-totter, drink pink
from yard-long glasses

Everyone wants me to sample
something then make me pay
Men bar my way clicking

cards for escort services
When women do the same
it feels like betrayal

Inside each giant temple
pilgrims in constant flux
pull suitcases on wheels, hump

backpacks or shopping bags, skirting
obstacles like ants waving antennae
seeking out sweetness

All paths lead through casinos
clockless havens of smoke and mirrors
A weary punter sleeps in his chair

Beneath ceilings painted à la Sistine Chapel
showgirls glitter at crooning gondoliers
fountains romp amongst orange groves

minstrels meander, stilt walkers stagger
adding zest to pizzas and giving jaded diners
a chance to digest their losses

The nearest thing to a meadow
is a swimming pool embedded
in mock grass

Burrows

Autumn rains have polished the paddocks
to a green sheen, tempting any rabbits
who've escaped pindone poison
to venture from their burrows

They nibble grass with gourmet delicacy
watching over their shoulders
ready to dash as my feet
trample the gravel

Down on the shopping strip
we, too, are digging burrows
to accommodate car parks and
foundations for eight-storey buildings

People will live above the shops
emerging from their warrens to nibble
and dash, choking on fumes
in the thickening traffic

A miasma will fill their burrows, rising
through stark black-and-white kitchens
poisoning the people
No white scuts to alert them to danger

Detachment

In the dream I'm walking down a lane
A squall of wind inveigles me
to lean into it and take comfort
Clouds fragment to a storyline I can't decipher

A few red leaves snatched from a maple
drift down and nest at my feet
A feather from a frazzled pigeon oscillates
on its voyage to the pavement

A loose tile plummets, shattering in my footsteps
Dustbins surrender their lids
Raucous cockatoos bite pine cones
suck the sap, and toss down the remnants willy-nilly

Bones fly over the fence from the playground
I wrap them conspiratorially
and hide them behind a lamp post
Now the wind eddies around me

whistling its tuneless menace
A clump of hair vanishes on an updraught
a tooth dislodges with a crack and flakes of skin
slough off in a whirling funnel

Ideas spring from my head, swarm briefly
then join the melee. Everything I hold
and everything I am is whisked away
I watch myself from a distance

Apocalypse

I just need a small shelf to rest on
amongst the throng surging along the street
lifting me off my feet
A refuge from the turbulent current
and the litter that never lets up

Maybe I'll find a crevice between walls
where warm air swirls around me
There I can watch the antics of the crowd
without bruising encounters

Barricades banish me from the footpath
in favour of cranes flaunting enormity
over scraps of land where heritage
bows to the tower block

I gaze up at crows wheeling
waiting to swoop on anything edible
any glitter of sunlight on silver

Still the people keep coming
Nobody listens to the bell's toll

The Wheelbarrow

With a nod to William Carlos Williams

No trace of red on this wheelbarrow
A glaze of rain water has rusted
the yellow handles
No white chickens either

A white cockatoo in the plum tree
plucks the sweet fruit meant for breakfast
throws down a kernel to bounce off
the galvanised iron body

The plants it once carried
are now taking over
Nothing depends on this wheelbarrow
except a lone spider

Swan Song

I know these leaves are dying
but their rich blood red
looks so much like vibrant life
spread in a blush

In the autumn of life a woman
with swollen and knotted fingers
knits a grandchild's jacket
in feather-soft white wool

A man on his deathbed
forgives his enemies, agrees
to donate his heart to the brother
he has hated for most of his life

A dying star turns supernova
the massive explosion of colour
seducing artists and seeding life
into darkness

www.ingramcontent.com/pod-product-compliance
Lightning Source LLC
Chambersburg PA
CBHW070925080526
44589CB00013B/1434